1 MONTH OF FREE READING

at

www.ForgottenBooks.com

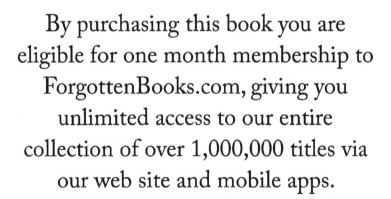

By purchasing this book you are eligible for one month membership to ForgottenBooks.com, giving you unlimited access to our entire collection of over 1,000,000 titles via our web site and mobile apps.

To claim your free month visit: www.forgottenbooks.com/free754283

ISBN 978-0-483-13530-7
PIBN 10754283

For support please visit www.forgottenbooks.com

Teaching of Religion

By REV. P. C. YORKE, D. D.

AN ADDRESS DELIVERED AT THE ANNUAL CONVENTION OF THE CATHOLIC EDUCATIONAL ASSOCIATION, AT SAN FRANCISCO, CALIFORNIA, TUESDAY, JULY 23, 1918.

SAN FRANCISCO:
THE TEXT BOOK PUBLISHING COMPANY
675 Stevenson Street
1918

Gift of
Rev. Ralph Hunt

Imprimatur
✠ ED. J. HANNA, D. D.
Metrop., S. F., Cal.

Teaching of Religion

By REV. P. C. YORKE, D. D.

AN ADDRESS DELIVERED AT THE ANNUAL CONVENTION OF THE CATHOLIC EDUCATIONAL ASSOCIATION, AT SAN FRANCISCO, CALIFORNIA, TUESDAY, JULY 23, 1918.

IN our Church legislation concerning Catholic schools the chief reason given for their necessity is our duty to safeguard the faith and morals of the children. In this country and in our day there is another and a positive reason for the establishment of Catholic schools, namely, that without such schools we cannot teach religion at all. Hence, putting aside the intrinsic value of religion as the greatest thing in the world, and looking on the matter from the purely scholastic standpoint, the teaching of religion is the most important function of the Catholic school. Any Catholic school that does not give to the teaching of religion at least the same care, the same skill and the same efficiency that it gives to other subjects, is like the fig tree the Lord cursed, not only because it bears no fruit, but because its very verdure is a snare to the parents that trust it, and a fraud on the Church that maintains it.

Therefore, in taking up the subject of the "Teaching of Religion," I am deeply conscious of its importance on the one side, and on the other I realize my personal limitations in giving it adequate treatment. Many large books have been written on the subject, and more and larger books might well be written. I do not pretend to the pedagogical equipment necessary to produce such works, and, besides, on an occasion like this, a paper is limited both by the patience of the audience and the time at our disposal. For those reasons and others, I will confine myself to a plain, untechnical consideration of the problem as viewed by one who has no theories to propound and no particular methods to advocate, but is chiefly interested in the aim that the children under his care are taught religion, and are taught it as well as it should be taught.

6

I do not intend to discuss here the teaching of religion in High Schools and Universities. High School methods and University methods are entirely different from primary methods. The New Code of Church Discipline says in Canon 1373: *"Juventus quae medias vel superiores scholas frequentat, pleniore religionis doctrina excolatur, et locorum Ordinarii curent ut id fiat per sacerdotes zelo et doctrina praestantes."* That is to say, "The young people who attend High Schools and Universities shall receive fuller religious instruction, and the local Bishops shall see to it that such instruction is imparted by priests who are distinguished by their zeal and learning." The question of teaching religion, therefore, in High Schools and Universities is beyond the scope of this paper, and may be safely left to the departments of Pedagogy, which, in accordance with the decrees of the Third Plenary Council of Baltimore, are established in our ecclesiastical seminaries.

Neither will I inject myself into the controversy about the place and function of the

Seventh and Eighth Grades in our American schools. Your own experience shows you that the vast majority of our children are content with six grades schooling, even if they go as far. The children who remain for the Seventh and Eighth Grades usually have the intention of passing into a High School of some sort. Therefore, the character of the instruction to be given them in religion, as in other subjects, should be conformed to the changing capabilities of the adolescent mind. Hence, it will make for clearness if I circumscribe the object of this paper still more closely and confine it to the teaching of religion in the elementary grades, or, as we used to say in old times, to the preparation of the children for the Sacraments.

With this purpose in view, let us now consider briefly:

    I.   What must we teach the children?

    II.   How should we teach it to them?

    III.   What are the chief aids or instruments at our disposal in teaching?

I.

In the first place, it is not very difficult to discover how much religious instruction the Church wishes us to impart to the children at this stage of their education. The theologians give us the minimum requirements when they explain the material object of faith and enumerate the truths we are bound to know and believe. Then the ecclesiastical authorities have put forth certain manuals commonly called Catechisms, and require a knowledge of the Christian Doctrine contained therein. These Catechisms, therefore, contain what we may call the average amount the average child should be supposed to know.

The great Jesuit theologian, Lehmkuhl, in his "Moral Theology," numbers 276 to 284, treats of the necessity of faith as far as concerns the objects to be believed. I will make a summary of his teaching, so that we may have before our eyes the very skeleton, as it were, of Christian instruction. He is, of course, writing not a school program, but is laying down practical rules for the guid-

9

ance of confessors who must be satisfied in dealing with uneducated penitents if they can get the irreducible minimum.

He first calls attention to the fact that there are certain truths which we must know and believe if we are to have any faith at all, such as, for instance, the existence of God. These truths, and how far they extend, do not concern us, because they are covered by the second class of truths which we must know and believe, because we are so commanded by Christ and His Church. These truths are grouped round the venerable ecclesiastical formulae known as the Apostles' Creed, the Lord's Prayer, the Ten Commandments and the Seven Sacraments. He says that there is a grave obligation, that is to say, an obligation binding under penalty of mortal sin, to know the substance of the things contained in the Apostles' Creed, the Lord's Prayer and the Ten Commandments. He doubts if there is a grave obligation to know the Our Father by heart. He asserts that to know the Creed by heart binds under pain of venial sin. The same holds of the Ten Commandments, but with even a lighter sanction. As to the Sacraments, we are strictly bound to know those whose reception is necessary, such as Penance, Holy Eucharist, and, in certain cases, Baptism. As to the others, we should learn about them when we come to receive them.

Lehmkuhl then develops those statements in more detail, taking up the Apostles' Creed article by article.

FIRST ARTICLE. *I believe in God.* We must believe explicitly that there is one God, and that in this God there are three persons, each of whom is God. That there are not three gods, but only one God. That the three persons are called the Father, the Son, and the Holy Ghost.

The Father Almighty, Creator of heaven and earth. We must explicitly believe in the creation of all things, and consequently in the omnipotence of God.

SECOND ARTICLE. *And in Jesus Christ, His only Son, our Lord.* We must believe explicitly that Jesus Christ is both God and Man. As God He is equal to His Father in all things. He is only one person, but belief in this point is sufficiently assured as long as the Nestorian heresy is not held.

THIRD ARTICLE. *Who was conceived by the Holy Ghost.* The miraculous conception is certainly to be held explicitly, but whether under pain of mortal sin is doubtful.

Born of the Virgin Mary. The perpetual virginity of the B. V. Mary is also to be believed explicitly, but the gravity of the obligation is doubtful.

FOURTH ARTICLE. *Suffered under Pontius Pilate, crucified—dead—and buried.* We must know, under penalty of mortal sin, both the fact of our Saviour's death and the manner in which it happened, namely, by crucifixion. As to Pontius Pilate, there is no reason to trouble the consciences of uneducated persons if they are not acquainted with this circumstance. To know the fact of the burial does not bind *sub gravi;* as they say, that is under pain of mortal sin.

FIFTH ARTICLE. *He descended into hell.* The same may be said of this circumstance as of the burial.

The third day He rose again from the dead. We must explicitly believe in the resurrection under penalty of mortal sin, but the circumstance of time, namely, that He rose the third day is not of the same gravity.

SIXTH ARTICLE. *He ascended into heaven, sitteth at the right hand of God, the Father Almighty.* It is sufficient for the uneducated to believe that Christ reigns in heaven with a glory proper to Him as the God-Man.

SEVENTH ARTICLE. *From thence he shall come to judge the living and the dead.* There is a grave obligation to know that Christ will hold the general judgment. What is understood by "the living and the dead" is harder to define explicitly.

EIGHTH ARTICLE. *I believe in the Holy Ghost.* This dogma is covered by the First Article.

NINTH ARTICLE. *The Holy Catholic Church.* We are strictly bound to know the necessity of remaining in the Catholic Church.

The Communion of Saints. We should know in a general way that the faithful form one body. There is a venial obligation to know that we can be helped by the saints in heaven, and that we can help the souls in Purgatory.

TENTH ARTICLE. *The forgiveness of sins.* There is a grave obligation to know how we can obtain forgiveness of sins in the Church through Baptism or Penance received either actually or by desire.

ELEVENTH ARTICLE. *The resurrection of the body.* We must explicitly believe *sub gravi* that the dead rise again.

TWELFTH ARTICLE. *And the life everlasting.* We must believe explicitly, under penalty of mortal sin, that there is an everlasting reward for the good in supernatural blessedness, and that there is an endless punishment for the wicked.

In the same manner we should know THE TEN COMMANDMENTS and believe in them, so that, if asked, we should be able to tell what things are commanded and forbidden by them. This does not hold as to the more remote conclusions to be drawn from the Decalogue, but only of those precepts that are formally mentioned therein or may be easily deduced therefrom. We are also bound to know the common PRECEPTS OF THE CHURCH.

As to the LORD'S PRAYER, writers commonly acknowledge that there is some kind of an obligation to know it by heart. The faithful also should be able to elicit acts of faith, hope, charity and contrition, though there is no strict obligation to have a set form of words . It is also becoming to add the Hail Mary to the Our Father, though it is not certain that it is a venial sin not to have it committed to memory, unless indeed such want of knowledge arises from criminal carelessness.

With regard to THE SACRAMENTS: we should know the Sacrament of Penance, both as a matter of precept and as a means for restoring grace.

We should know about the real presence of our Lord in the Eucharist, and that it is also a sacrifice by assisting at which we fulfill the divine and ecclesiastical law.

This is, as I have said before, the very skeleton and anatomy of Christian Doctrine, and if we wish to find what Church authority requires of the average child we must go to the Catechisms.

The old classic Catechisms written in the English language fall into two families. One family opens with the question, "Who made you?" the other opens with the question, "Who made the world?" The chief representatives of the first family are the Catechism, said to have been prepared by order of the First Plenary Council of Baltimore, and the Catechism in use in Great Britain. The chief representatives of the second class are Butler's Catechism, the Maynooth Catechism and the so-called Baltimore Catechism. The Catechisms of the first type contain about 370 questions, while the Catechisms of the second type contain over 420. Many of these questions, however are merely rhetorical, introducing or closing a subject, while others are just ligature or liaison questions used in passing from one subject to another.

The chief characteristic of the first type is

that the doctrine is pinned on, so to speak, to the formulae. We have first Faith treated under the twelve articles of the Apostles' Creed. Then we have Hope heading an explanation of the Our Father and Hail Mary. The third part is scheduled under Charity, and deals with the Commandments and Precepts. Then follows the doctrine on the Sacraments, and the Catechism closes with a summary of the Virtues and Vices, the Christian's Daily Exercise and a Rule of Life.

In the second class of Catechisms the teaching follows much the same line, but it is divorced from the Articles of the Apostles' Creed. This divorce is most evident in the Baltimore Catechism, which also inserts the doctrine on the Sacraments before the Ten Commandments and entirely eliminates the exposition of the Our Father.

To sum up, therefore, the answer to our first question, What must we teach the children? we may use the words of the Encylical of Pius X on the teaching of Christian Doctrine: "As the things divinely revealed are so many and so various that it is no easy task either to acquire a knowledge of them, or to retain them in memory, our predecessors have very wisely reduced the pith and marrow of this saving doctrine to four distinct heads: The Apostles' Creed, the Sacraments, the Ten Commandments and the Lord's Prayer. In the doctrine of the Creed are contained all things which are to be held according to the discipline of the Christian Faith, whether they regard the knowledge of God, or the creation and government of the world, or the redemption of the human race, or the rewards of the good and the punishments of the wicked. The doctrine of the Seven Sacraments comprehends the signs, and, as it were, the instruments for obtaining divine grace. In the Decalogue is laid down whatever has reference to the Law the end whereof is charity. Finally, in the Lord's Prayer is contained whatever can be desired, hoped or salutarily prayed for by men. It follows that these four commonplaces, as it were, of Sacred Scripture being explained, there can scarcely be wanting anything to be learned by a Christian man."

II.

Having thus gained from the moral theologians, the Catechisms and the Pope a general idea of the amount of Christian Doctrine the average child is supposed to learn, let us now pass to the second question and consider how that knowledge is to be imparted.

Here it will be useful to call to our minds the reason why we are instructing the children in Christian Doctrine. Certainly all will agree that it is not merely to give them an acquaintance with a set of speculative truths. Our end is to fit them to live real Christian lives and save their souls. Even religious knowledge alone will not save them, nor yet faith alone. The Apostle says: "The devils believe and tremble." Religion is not only a truth, but it is a way and a life. From the very beginning of their school days, we must take care that the children are living their religion.

According to the best pedagogical practice, the children learn by doing. Good conduct must be established, the Sacraments must be frequented, Mass must be attended, prayers must be said regularly, and, according to their age, all those habits or practices must be inculcated that in after years will be the mainstay of an upright life. Above all, we must remember that the fear of the Lord is the beginning of wisdom, and that, while there are many dangers in trying to make children devout, there is no danger especially amongst us in trying to make them reverent.

In his letter to the convention of this Association held at Detroit, Pope Piux X said: "To one principal and supreme point we would call your attention as you meet in your annual convention to discuss the perfecting of Christian training. Each of you should be persuaded that he renders to this enterprise a real service only in so far as he imitates Christ, who, when about to deliver to the world His heavenly doctrine, 'began to do and to teach.' Hence it is by personal example, no less than by other social agencies, that each one of you should further the cause of Catholic education. Example, indeed, is mighty to persuade, nor is there any better means of moving mankind to the practice of virtue. Quite particularly is this true in the education of children who are all the readier to imitate what they behold in proportion as their judgment is weak."

It is a pleasant thing to be able to boast that in the matter of these recommendations of Pius X our American tradition is excellent. No matter how we may have been criticised for other things, every one admits the splendid example of our religious teachers, and even outsiders recognize in the very manners of our school children the refining influence exercised, especially by the Sisters on the pupils they are instructing unto justice.

Coming now to the task of informing the child's intellect with the necessary truths, we find that in this matter, as in so many others, the Church has her own method. It would indeed be strange if an organization sent out by divine authority to make disciples of all the nations had not developed a system of teaching in her long history. That system is known as the Catechesis. Like so many other things, it was taken over from the synagogue and brought to a high pitch of efficiency in the Catechumenate. It survived all the disasters of the downfall of civilization, and, though since the invention of printing, it has suffered a comparative decline, the ecclesiastical authorities have never ceased urging it as the proper method of instruction in Christian Doctrine, not only for children, but also for adults, and the New Code of Canon Law declares that it is the peculiar and most weighty office of the pastors of souls to provide for the catechetical instruction of the Christian people (No. 1329).

The word Catechesis comes from the Greek, and meant originally to teach orally or by word of mouth. Essentially it consists of three elements—oral instruction, questions put by the teacher, questions put by the pupil. There is a perfect example of Catechesis in the finding of our Lord in the temple. St. Luke tells us that He was sitting in the midst of the teachers hearing them and asking them questions, and that all were astonished at His wisdom and His answers. Here you have the three elements

—first, the exposition by the teachers; second, the answer by the pupil, and, third, the pupil's questions put to the teachers.

I should like here to guard you against confounding the Catechesis with what is known as the Socratic method. In the Catechesis the emphasis is laid on the instruction; in the Socratic method the emphasis is laid on the question. The object of Socrates was so to order his interrogations that facts and principles already in the mind of his disciple should lead of themselves to the conclusion he wished to draw forth. But in revealed religion all the Socratic questions in the world could not extract from the human intellect the doctrine of the Trinity, for instance, or the fact of the Incarnation. Such truths must be taught to the hearer and taught with authority. There are, it is true, doctrines written on the fleshly tablets of our hearts that may in a way be reached by the Socratic method, but even in the case of such doctrines we need the authority of revelation to establish them so that they may be known adequately, decisively and without the aberrations that seem to pursue the unaided attempts of human reason at setting up a satisfactory moral code.

The method of the Catechesis, then, is the method of authority. This is especially true in the case of the young children with whom we are dealing. They have in them a natural disposition to believe. They will take your word without thought of questioning it. There is no need of seeking reasons from biology or analogies from zoology to prove to them that God is good or that Providence takes care of them. It is simply a waste of time to torture them with Socratic questions to demonstrate that they should not lie when the mere proposition of the commandment is sufficient to make them accept the obligation. These truths, of course, require amplification and illustration, but they do not need argument. In fact, children in these grades are incapable of ratiocination in such subjects. The time will come when their reason will function, and function acutely, and then the method of the Catechesis must change, but at this stage of our children's education, our model is our Lord, who spake not as scribe and Pharisee, but as one having authority.

What, after all, are the chief mental assets the little ones have in coming to us at this period of their lives. They are, as you know, the memory and the imagination. Therefore, our main object must be to use the memory and to inform the imagination. *Pari passu* with this will go a development of the intellect and of the will, but the immediate means at our hand are the power of recollection and the power of exercising the fancy.

Now, the ideal of the Catechesis at this time is to bring the faculties of the child and the faculties of the teacher into perfect tune. Therefore, the teacher must learn to become again a little child to attain the end of bringing the children into the kingdom of heaven. This is by no means an easy thing to do, nor is it to be attained in a day or a year. It demands serious discipline in the novitiate, and it demands serious preparation for every class. The year's work must be carefully organized, the day's work must be carefully put together. There are various systems or methods of Catechesis which you will find described in books. I am not an advocate of strict or hidebound systems or methods, and I believe every good teacher will put her own personality into whatever system is adopted. Moreover, I believe very strongly that the various teaching orders should be loyal to the traditions of their communities, for it will be usually found that those who shaped those communities had a special genius for teaching and handed on to their children precepts and practices of real pedagogical value.

III.

Let us now come to the third question and speak of the chief aids or instruments at our disposal in the teaching of religion. These aids or instruments are many, but in practice the most important is the Catechism.

1. (a) The Catechism is a book containing a certain number of stereotyped questions and answers. The pupil is given so many answers to get off by heart, and when the teacher puts the question he gives back

the answer in the exact words of the book. This style of presenting knowledge was very popular in the middle of the last century, and we had catechisms on all kinds of subjects—history, botany, chemistry, civics and so on. The fashion has passed away almost completely as far as secular subjects are concerned, but it is still jealously retained in the teaching of religion.

Of the former class of Catechisms, J. G. Fitch writes very severely:.

"To print a book of questions and answers is to assume that there is to be no real contact of thought between scholar and master, that all the questions which are to be asked are to take one particular form, and they all admit of but one answer. There is no room for inquisitiveness on the part of the learner, nor for digression on the part of the teacher, no room for the play of the intelligence of either around the subject in hand; the whole exercise has been devised to convert a study which ought to awaken intelligence, into a miserable mechanical performance; and two people who ought to be in intimate intellectual relations with each other, into a brace of impostors—the one teaching nothing, the other learning nothing, but both acting a part and reciting somebody else's words out of a book."— Lectures on Teaching, p. 141.

It is true there may be schools where these words describe what happens in religious instruction. Even so, that would not be sufficient reason to advocate the abolition of the religious Catechism. Wherever you find in a great organization like the Church a practice common to various countries and ages you usually discover that it represents the practical meeting of some real need or the solution of some problem. In the old times there were no Catechisms such as we have now, but from the very beginning we find formulae and stereotyped questions and answers. Our Lord Himself gave us a form of prayer. In spite of the learned men I am convinced that the Apostles made the Apostles' Creed. The question and answer are imbedded in the ritual of Baptism and considering the origin of the Christian Church it would be strange if it were not so, seeing how it is imbedded in that most ancient ceremony, the Passover supper of the Jews.

Then from the very beginning there was tampering with the Christian doctrine. To meet this tampering the Church was most particular as to the terms in which she clothed her "sound doctrine." St. Paul admonishes Timothy to avoid profane novelties of words and to "hold the form of sound words which thou hast heard of me." As the great heresies swept through Christendom the Councils of the Church defined with more and more exactness what Christians should believe. Highly technical expressions came into use and at one time the whole world was split in two over the smallest letter in the Greek alphabet.

It was to furnish the faithful with the form of sound words that after the invention of printing, and especially after the rise of Protestantism, Catechisms were issued by competent authority. Those catechisms not only contained the doctrines that had been defined, but also furnished on their own responsibility accurate explanations of other teachings which form, as is were, the *pomoerium fidei,* an outer defense for dogma.

The Catholic respect, therefore, for the form of sound words and the Catholic distrust for heretical inaccuracy, not mental sluggishness nor fear of progress, is the reason why we have retained the Catechism in religious instruction when it has been abandoned in secular subjects. We must also remember that the duty of teaching Catechism devolves on others besides priests and teachers. Parents and guardians, and all in charge of children, are bound to teach it either personally or by others, and an authoritative elementary manual containing the things to be taught and cast in the form of question and answer will always be of use and necessity.

But at the same time we must remember that in the Catechesis the Catechism is only a tool and a guide, and that the real work is done by the oral instruction. The ideal of the Catechesis is that the minds of the teacher and of the pupil must be in perfect tune. The teacher not only propounds the doctrine, but illustrates it, analyses it, puts it one way now, another way again, and uses in fact every device of the teaching art, even as our Lord Himself instructed His disciples. Then by means of frequent questions the catechist holds their attention, clears their misapprehensions, systematizes their thoughts, insists on the form of sound words, and, finally, as all teaching consists in getting the pupil's mind to work for itself, encouraging the use of questions from the pupil's side to meet his difficulties and round out his knowledge.

(*b*) The question now arises, What Catechism should we use? In this matter we have no choice. The Bishop is the teaching authority in his diocese, and it is his privilege to prescribe the Catechism or other books to be used by his flock. Canon 1336 of the new code says: *"Ordinarii loci est omnia in sua diocesi edicere quae ad populum in Christina doctrina instituendum spectent; et etiam religiosi exempti quoties non exemptos docent eadem servare tenentur."* It belongs to the local Ordinary to regulate for his diocese all things that concern the instruction of the people in

Christian doctrine; and even exempt religious are bound to observe those regulations when they are teaching persons not exempt.

In reply to those teachers who may chafe at this restriction of their liberty to use a text book that they are more familiar with or that they may consider more effective than the local Catechism I might say that here in America we are inclined to lay too much stress on the text book. This is preeminently the land of text books. We have employed our best talent in compiling them and have spent millions of money in producing them. Great corporations strive for the patronage of the schools, public and private, and the battle of the book agents rages all over the country, so that in some States the government has been compelled to step in and manufacture a series of its own.

Yet, of the three things in a school—the teacher, the child and the text book—the least important is the text book. I will not elaborate this idea here, but will refer you to the Report of Superintendent of Schools of the Archdiocese of San Francisco for

1916-1917, page 33, where the Rev. Ralph
Hunt ably discusses the qualifications of the
teacher. You will see from the nature of
the Catechesis itself that this is especially
true of religious instruction. Yet there has
been no text book which has been so sav-
agely criticised as the Catechism. Bishop
Bellord went so far as to speak of our failure in religious instruction, and ascribed it
to the imperfect manner in which our Catechisms in common use are constructed. He
might have got away with it, as they say, if
Satan had not tempted him to write a Catechism of his own, and Job's wish was grati-
fied, "Oh, that mine enemy would write a
book." In my humble opinion Bellord's
Catechism is about as bad as a Catechism
could be.

The drawback they must meet who try to
write a Catechism is that they have to satisfy
two classes of critics, the theologians on the
one side and the teachers on the other. The
theologians demand scientific accuracy and
completeness, while the teachers are looking
for brevity and simplicity. But we must
remember that we are teaching religion, not

theology, and that we are dealing with children, not with professional students of university grade. On the other hand, we must guard the form of sound words and realize the depth of the riches of the wisdom and of the knowledge of God. My idea of a good Catechism is one that contains the traditional amount of information, in which the definitions are accurately expressed as far as they go, and in which the language is not only correct but rhythmic and elevated. However, we have to face facts, and even if the Catechism is not the best attainable, as long as it is prescribed by authority the teacher must use it. This compulsion, too, need not interfere with the efficiency of the instruction. It has been well said that a poor text book becomes a challenge to a good teacher to make up for its deficiencies by personal work. An unsatisfactory Catechism may stimulate the conscientious instructor to that oral teaching which is the very soul of the Catechesis.

(c) There is another question connected with the Catechism which you may well ask me—Should we require the children to memorize the answers word for word? Here, as you know, there is a difference of opinion as to the theory and a difference in practice. It is not necessary to go into the reasons for and against, because, as a matter of fact, the wise superior will find out what the pastor wants and will govern her conduct accordingly. This much, however, I would advise that where there are several priests teaching or examining the children they should be asked to have one system. If the word for word test is required all should require it; if it is not required, then no individual should insist on it.

In this connection I would impress upon you the necessity of accuracy in memorizing the prayers, the various formulae and the dogmatic definitions. It would be ludicrous if it were not so sad to listen to the perversions the most sacred words suffer in the mouths of children who are badly taught. They are reciting those forms every day, apparently the teacher is listening to them, and yet to judge by what they do articulate they have as much meaning to them as "eena, meena, mina, mo."

There are two remedies for this state of affairs. First, to teach the form correctly in the beginning and of this I will speak later on when I come to the question of reading. Second, frequently to test the accuracy of the children's memory by means of writing. I would recommend this exercise to you: The first days of school the teacher usually has to find some "busy work" for the pupils while she reorganizes her class. Without any warning to the children, give them the task of writing out from memory the common prayers like the Our Father. Then take the results into some quiet place alone and read them. If you have a due sense of the dignity of religion you will most likely go down on your knees, strike your breast and cry *mea culpa, mea maxima culpa.*

At the end of the year, again without warning, give the same task to the children, compare the two sets of papers, and you will have before you the most searching criticism possible of your work during the past year.

2. Practical teachers will admit that one

of the most efficacious aids in imparting instruction is the careful grading of the subject matter. This is as true of religion as it is of other branches of knowledge. St. Paul himself speaks of milk for babes and strong meat for men. The old North Italian Catechism, a revision of which was adopted by Pius X as the official Catechism of the Province of Rome, consists of three stages or grades. The first contains "elementary truths for children of a tender age," the second is the Catechism for pupils preparing for the Sacraments and the third is destined for the so-called continuation classes, corresponding in amount of matter to the large Deharbe. In ungraded Catechisms like Butler's and the Baltimore, a common practice in some school programs is to apportion for the first grade a certain number of chapters beginning with Chapter I and continuing through the various grades to the end of the book. Thus, for instance, in Grade I the children are taught Chapters I to IV; in Grade II, Chapters V to XII, and so on. This is the method in almost universal use in Sunday Schools. The children begin the Catechism five or six times and tunnel their way to light and freedom only just before they receive the Sacraments.

Now, as against this practice there are two arguments that are conclusive. First, there are truths at the end of the Catechism that children even in the First Grade should know. Take the question of good conduct alone, without which all our teaching is dead and profitless. In our Baltimore Catechism the Commandments of God and the Church form the last part of the book; and while, no doubt, the child learns the substance of them indirectly in the very first years of his schooling, yet their formal inculcation is postponed to what for so many children is the end of their religious education; second, the late legislation on the communion of children has worked a revolution in the matter to be presented even to the youngest child. From the very beginning the Eucharist and penance enter into their program. It is true the requirements for the early grades are few and simple, but the subjects are there and must be treated.

When we add to these thoughts the further consideration that there are answers in the early chapters of the Catechism that are, I will not say beyond the comprehension of Second Grade pupils, but beyond even their powers of articulation, we will readily see how helpful it would be to pick out the questions concerning the necessary truths first and then add to them year by year until the whole Catechism is mastered. Inasmuch as in most States we have compulsory education, at least as far as the normal Sixth Grade, there is no reason why we should not provide a graded five-year course in Christian Doctrine, as is done in the well-known Salford Catechisms. The whole Baltimore Catechism could be covered in these five years by assigning two new questions a week, thus giving plenty of opportunity for an extended Catechesis even in crowded class rooms, and above all providing for that steady repetition of old and fundamental matter which is the very essence of successful teaching in this, as in all other subjects.

3. From the very beginning of her his-

tory the Church has used the art of painting in teaching religion. The art of sculpture came later, but both were employed for the same purpose—to convey to the believer the great truths of the faith. Hence we would naturally expect to find the picture or the image rated high as an aid to teaching. Up to not so many years ago good pictures were scarce, dear and hard to obtain, but now-a-days, in consequence of the progress made in the various reproduction processes, a teacher has at hand a veritable store of beautiful copies of the masterpieces of art, both plain and in colors and at a moderate cost.

Here let me digress for a moment and insist on the great advantage it will be to a teacher to begin from the very first years of her career to collect her own teaching apparatus and to keep a note book.

By her teaching apparatus I do not mean the furniture proper to every school room, but a more personal and intimate collection of objects which she has found useful and stimulating in working out the method of teaching she has colored with her own qualities. Pictures, old Christmas cards,

advertising specimens, clippings from cata-
logues, magazines and newspapers, dolls
dressed to show the vestments, postals, cray-
ons and a score of other things, if kept together in a special box will be found most
useful to illustrate the instruction, to serve
as stimuli for expression work, to stir up
interest in the class and to be given as prizes
to provoke emulation.

The teacher will find her note book a most
precious record of her mental development and a most helpful adjunct in preparing for her daily task. I know, of course,
there are those who will smile at the idea
of preparation in connection with the Catechism lesson, but they are not of the seed
through which salvation is wrought in
Israel. There is no lesson that requires
such careful, nay meticulous, preparation
as the daily instruction in religion. For
myself, being unprepared, I should sooner
undertake to address a class of theologians
on the Syncatabasis than take half an hour's
catechism in the baby grade. Now, we
know by experience that we do not always
come to the preparation of our lessons with

the same minds. At times we are bright and alert, the ideas sparkle spontaneously, the words flow, the subject stands out in sharp detail; at other times we are dull and stupid and tired, our thoughts are wandering and our studies are a weariness to body and soul. If in the latter case, however, you have in your note book a record of the preparation of the lesson the year before when you were fine and fit, especially if you make it a practice after school to set down the thoughts and illustrations that come to you out of the white heat of teaching, you will have the very best aid possible to overcome the deadness that besets you and the most stimulating of all motives to equal your past performance.

Let us return to the picture lesson. It is in the preparation of the picture lesson that one sees most clearly the advantages of the note book. Here again the wise men may elevate their eyebrows and sneer at the foolishness of preparing a picture lesson. Is it not the business of a picture to speak for itself? No attitude could be more superficial. We see in a picture only what we bring to it, and it is the task of the teachers so to furnish the minds of the children that they may recognize according to their capacity the vision the artist saw and bodied forth by cunning brush from glowing palette for the delight and instruction of men.

For example, let us take the subject so favored by painters and so loved by little ones—Christ and the children. The teacher in preparing this lesson will naturally have two ends in view—to see the scene as it actually happened and to make the children see it for themselves. First, then, the teacher turns to the Gospels and finds in St. Matthew his account of the incident. At the foot of the page she will notice that the same incident is recorded in St. Mark and St. Luke. Let her now make three parallel columns in her note book and write in them the three accounts under their respective authors' names. A study of what she has written will show her that while the backbone of the story is identical in the three accounts, each of the evangelists gives some trait or circumstance that the others omit.

Now let the teacher go to the Community library and take down that most excellent Life of Christ by Father Maas, S. J. It is what they call a Diatessaron, that is to say, the four Gospels are woven into one continuous narrative. Moreover, it is furnished with a sufficiency of reliable and learned notes. Let the teacher copy into her note book at the foot of the parallel columns the account of the incident as he blends it from the synoptics. Let her also study his notes carefully and enter a few key words to remind her of the time, the place, the occasion of the incident and of the manners and customs of the people. Finally, let her get one or more of what I might call the literary lives of Christ, such as Fouard's or Elliot's and write into her note book their description of the scene incorporating, as they do, not only the facts, but also the geography, the scenery, the architecture, the popular ways, the historical and personal allusions to make a concrete picture. Then having done all this, let the teacher make it the matter of her morning meditation for the next week. Little by little the scene will begin to live for her. As when we are trying for the proper focus in projecting a picture the blurred and indistinct image trembles at first and then begins to take shape and form and at last stands out in clear and sharp definition, so the confused outlines of the story will begin to co-ordinate themselves and we shall see the Judean village and the flat-roofed houses glaring white under the brilliant sky. We shall see the narrow street and the loungers in the shade stirred from their lethargy by the approach of the Prophet of Nazareth and His little band. We shall see how our Lord retires into one of the houses and mark the constant stream of visitors coming and going and listen to the murmur of the high arguments that have made memorable that humble abode. At last, as the burden of the day is broken and the tempered heats render tolerable the next stage of their journey, our Lord and His Apostles appear in the village street and make ready to depart. The strain of the day is evident in His lined face and drooping shoulders and the journey before them is long. The Apostles gather about Him in loving sympathy and cast in their minds how to lighten His way. At this very moment the Mothers of the village, hearing that the great Rabbi is about to leave them, snatch up their children and run to demand what is their right by immemorial custom, the blessing of the Holy Man for their little ones. We can see the thunder frown on the brows of James and John, we can hear the flying word from the impetuous lips of Peter, we can mark the astonished mothers hurt and indignant at this more than Galilean rudeness. Then we fix our gaze upon our Lord. He turns his eyes flaming with anger upon His Apostles, with bitterness He rebukes His own. He bids them stand aside and make way for the children. He seats Himself. The children run to Him. They cluster round His knees. They climb into His lap. They hang over His shoulders. He lays His hands upon them and blesses them and, like the sound of music dropping from the stars, we hear His words: "Suffer the little children to come unto Me and forbid them not, for of such is the Kingdom of God."

4. Especially in our day when everybody is able to read, the art of reading as an aid to religious instruction has a very great extension. It comprehends everything from the unchangeable word of God in the Holy Scriptures to the ephemeral product of the periodical press. It would take a treatise to do full justice to the subject and therefore here I can only touch on a few points more intimately connected with school discipline. Even in this restricted sphere I would refer you to my paper, read at the Milwaukee meeting of this Association, on the Educational Value of Christian Doctrine, for a more extended explanation of the place of reading in religious instruction. I leave aside also the vexed question of the so-called Catholic Readers and will confine myself to a few practical points more intimately connected with the Catechism.

(a) As you will gather from the Milwaukee paper, we all have two vocabularies —the vocabulary of daily life and the vocabulary of books or literature. We may divide the latter vocabulary into secular and religious. The child in the first grade who knows the common prayers and has been told the stories of the Infancy and Passion of Our Lord is using a vocabulary of at least 800 words, of which a large number are peculiar to religion.

Now, in acquiring the power of secular reading, that is, of recognizing and reproducing secular words, we employ certain systems of teaching. Some use a sight system, some a phonic system and some a combination of the two. But whatever system is used, the words are classified on a plan and so organized that the pupil passes from the known to the unknown, from the easy to the difficult combinations.

Unfortunately, however, in our published books we have no such classification or organization of the religious vocabulary. From secular readers, of course, religion is barred and I know no series of Catholic readers that has even attempted the task. In fact, a great many so-called Catholic readers are merely the secular readers ornamented with a few "holy pictures."

Hence, if the teacher wishes to get as good reading results from the religious vocabulary as from the secular vocabulary it will be necessary for her to make her own classification. It does not matter on what system she bases it, as the religious vocabulary also is English and subject to the same rules as the secular vocabulary.

(*b*) In teaching the pupils how to read the Catechism or any other religious text you may have at your disposal, always keep before your mind that you are teaching reading, not religion. Hence, the task should be undertaken in the reading period of the school day, not in the religion period. Whatever religious instruction the child will absorb in this exercise will come to it indirectly. Above all, if you have a doctrinal explanation text, beware of asking the children to memorise it. Such texts are intended first and foremost as reading lessons, not as tasks in Catechism.

(*c*) As I have mentioned above, reading and its fellow art, writing, are the great guarantees of accuracy. There are certain persons—even writers of Catechisms—who

49

believe that Christian Doctrine should be conveyed in words of one syllable and laugh to scorn the idea of proposing to children such polysyllables as Infallibility and Indefectibility. I notice, however, that the same gentlemen never blink an eye when the same children are required to know in arithmetic what is a multiplicand or a subtrahend or are punished if in geography they do not master such blessed words as Mesopotamia or Madagascar. After all, what is the child going to school for? Is it not precisely to be taught such things and why should we take for granted the necessity of instruction in the technical terms of profane learning and draw the line at instruction in the technical terms of religion?

In teaching Catechism the blackboard is as necessary and as useful as it is in teaching arithmetic. The children should not be permitted to face the new words in their Catechism or reader until the teacher has pronounced them, written them down and explained their meaning. Do not imagine that children find difficulty in long words only. In fact, polysyllables are not the hardest words in English. I have usually found more trouble in domesticating the monosyllabic "heir" that I have in harnessing "transubstantiation."

5. To treat adequately the place of Holy Scripture in religious instruction even in the early grades would require another treatise. Here again, in order to keep within due limits I would refer you to my Milwaukee paper for a fuller expression of what is in my mind. There are three practical points, however, to which I would call your attention.

(*a*) Bible history in the grades with which we are concerned cannot, of course, be taught as formal history. We must use it for two purposes—first to get the facts— to hear the story of the dealings of God with man. We begin with the Infancy of Our Lord, then we take up His Passion, Death, Resurrection and Ascension; afterwards we learn the chief events of His Public Ministry. In like manner we make a study of the main topics of the Old Testament, telling them as stories with only the slightest reference to chronology.

Our second purpose is to use the Bible History for the illustration of Christian Doctrine. Those of you who read the divine office will remember with what detail and with what ingenuity the Responds and the Lessons of the first nocturn from the Old Testament are made to typify and illustrate the teachings of the Church and even the events of Christian history. Again, in order to husband space I will refer you to Canon Glancey's introduction to Knecht's Practical Commentary on Holy Scripture, a book that should be in every school library and that no teacher can peruse without pleasure and profit.

(*b*) In telling the stories of the Bible to the children I would advise you to adopt the practice of using the Bible language. Of course, I know a great deal of fuss is made about our various translations into English, but bear in mind that there is no general authorized English version of the Scriptures for Catholics and that any translation that has the imprimatur of the Ordinary may be lawfully used. Moreover, the differences in the literary value of the versions have been greatly over emphasized. There is a style common to them all, inasmuch as they all come from the one original and it is that common style we wish to impress upon the children by giving them the Bible stories as far as possible in the Bible language.

(c) A third point I would recommend to teachers is to adopt a uniform system of pronouncing the proper names. In the Protestant version, known as the King James, these names were as a rule crudely transliterated from the Hebrew, with the result that after three centuries they have even to those familiar with the version a harsh and uncouth look. In the Catholic version they were worn down and polished by passing through the Greek Septuagint and the Latin Vulgate. Thus Hezekiah became Ezechias and Joshua, Jesus, while some of them suffered an English adaptation and we have Judah, Judas and Jude. Indeed, the King James revisers themselves did not dare to carry their system to its full conclusion and were instructed to leave the names in common use undisturbed, so that we have Moses not Mosheh in the Anglican Authorized Version.

For this reason we cannot use the English tradition of pronouncing the Biblical Proper Names and among ourselves there is no uniform practice. Even in reading the Sunday Epistle and Gospel one is likely to find three different pronunciations from the same pulpit on the same day. This diversity arises from sheer carelessness and is unjustifiable because there is a fairly standardized pronunciation for the names in the Anglo-Catholic versions.

6. Just as from the beginning the Church employed the art of painting in the teaching of religion, so also she employed the art of poetry. She took over from the synagogue the Songs of David and made them the nucleus of her official prayer book. As early as the Epistles of St. Paul we find fragments of hymns inspired by her own peculiar spirit and the Psalmi idiotici, such as the Gloria in Excelsis, the Te Deum, the Breastplate of St. Patrick and others showed how the songs the Apostles bade the Christians to sing in their hearts found expression

54

on fire touched lips. At the freedom of the Church there came a great outburst of rhymed and stressed melody associated with the name of St. Ambrose and culminating in magnificent sequences like the Dies Irae, the Stabat Mater and the Lauda Sion, which are to the literature of the Middle Age what the glorious Gothic Cathedrals are to the architecture of the same period.

Hymns fall into two classes, doctrinal hymns and devotional hymns. Of the latter I will merely say that their choice is a matter of taste and about tastes there is to be no disputing. As to doctrinal hymns, they have been always used—even by heretics—for popular teaching. Arius, anticipating the Salvation Army, embodied his heresies in songs adopted to the pot-house airs of Alexandria. In the Middle Age the whole Catechism was done into verse and you can find even today among Irish speakers stave after stave containing the full round of Christian Doctrine.

As to the singing of the hymns, an official tune book for the country is greatly to be desired, but there are two points that are even now easily attainable. First, in the same school have a common exact musical text and, second, the teaching of the hymns as music belongs to the music period.

7. As my time is coming to a close I will refer you to my paper read at the Buffalo meeting for the value of the Liturgy as an instrument of teaching. As far as regards religious exercises and devotions, school Mass and school prayers, sodalities and the frequentation of the sacraments, I should prefer to leave these things to your Catholic instinct and the customs of your various localities. After all it is the Christian life that counts. Amid the hard realities of the world many of the sweet lessons our little pupils are learning shall dry up like the morning dew, but if the Mass remains and the Sacraments and the habit of prayer and the Commandments and the Charity that is the fulfilment of the law, then our teaching shall not have been in vain and the loyal children of Holy Church, their children and their children's children shall rise up and call us blessed.

Appendices.

For the convenience of teachers the extracts referred to in the body of the paper are printed hereinafter.

APPENDIX A.

A Manual of Instructions in Christian Doctrine, With an Introduction on Religious Instruction. Edited by the late Provost Wenham. Seventeenth edition. London: St. Anselm's Society. 1903. Pages ix, x, xi.:

Making the Importance of the Subject Apparent.—But while complete and accurate knowledge and skillful methods are necessary for success in teaching any subject, there are two points especially in which religious instruction requires treatment in a manner peculiar to itself. It has been shown how pre-eminently important it is. But it is not enough that the teacher should see this. Those who are taught must be made to see it. It must be made to appear in the manner of teaching it. The children must see that it is treated as the most important. With this object some give a longer time to religious instruction than to other matters. But this is dangerous, as, unless the instruction is very skillfully given, the additional call on the children's attention is apt to engender tedium. Nor is any great impression made by giving up to religious instruction the first hour of school, while there are not infrequently great inconveniences in this arrangement. But the importance of the subject will be impressed on the children's minds by their observing that this lesson is given with greater care than others, that more is made of proficiency in this than in other things in distributing praise and rewards, that dull, backward children are paid particular attention to in this subject; and, above all, that it is treated with reverence, not as one that must be "got up" in preparation for an examination or an inspection, but as one that is taught punctually and carefully at all times for its own sake.

Reverence.—Having spoken of reverence, it may be well to insist a little longer on the extreme importance of this beyond everything else. One would speak with diffidence; but it would seem that teachers often make a mistake in aiming at devotion in the children rather than reverence. For to make people devout is not in our power; and to aim

57

at it is dangerous, as leading, in some cases, to a sort of reaction against religion altogether, and in others to a sort of excitement which is taken for devotion, but which has has no solid foundation. But it is a proverb that "without reverence there is no religion," and there are no dangers attending the inculcation of this. On the contrary, it is the atmosphere which will still continue to support faith, even when morality is weakened. It will influence the wild and headstrong when nothing else can turn them, and is a good soil for the development of devotion.

Just let us observe how strictly this lesson of reverence was taught to men in old times by God himself: how Moses is warned to treat the very ground he stood on as holy, because of God's presence. When God would speak to His people, they were to sanctify themselves for three days, and Mount Sinai was hedged round to prevent their too near approach. He who blasphemed was to be stoned without mercy. None but the priests were allowed to enter into the Holy place of the Temple; none but the high priest into the Holy of Holies. The earth swallowed up those who would intrude into the priestly office. Oza was struck dead for only putting his hand to lay hold of the ark. Forty-two children were devoured by bears because they did not reverence the prophet of God; and for using the sacred vessels out of the Temple, King Baltasser was dethroned and slain, and his kingdom brought to an end. These and other examples show the value of a spirit of reverence in the sight of God. And as it had to be taught to the world of old before they could receive the teaching of our Lord, so it is the very soil in which alone faith lives and thrives. "The fear of the Lord is the beginning of wisdom." It should, then, be ceaselessly enforced by the teacher, both in word and example.

APPENDIX B.

Archdiocese of San Francisco, California. Second Annual Report of Superintendent of Schools. 1916-1917. Rev. Ralph Hunt:

The Teacher—

It may be a trite saying that "the teacher is the school," but it is not so sure that the significance of this obvious educational maxim is always recognized. At any rate, it is the fashion with educational systems nowadays to impose unnecessary restrictions on the teacher, and in general to subordinate his interests to the exigencies of the system. This is an inversion of the true order. The system exists for the teacher, not the teacher for the system. Text books, methods, curricula and all the paraphernalia used in teaching are simply the instruments in the teacher's hands, and, however well adapted to their purpose, will be only as effective as the teacher makes them. Every appliance depends for its success upon the intelligence with which it is used, and, just as the bungling mechanic, with the choicest tools, will botch his work, so too will the unskillful teacher fail even with the best of methods. Indeed, it will be admitted that the very perfection of the instrument, or the method, will in all such cases only enhance the failure. Hence, under whatever system or with whatever methods, the paramount factor in education will always be the teacher.

APPENDIX C.

Catholic Educational Association. Bulletin, Vol. IV, No. 1. Report of the Proceedings and Addresses of the Fourth Annual Meeting, Milwaukee, Wis., July 8-11, 1907. Pages 239-243:

In the elementary school the first of all the studies is language. The child is taught to read and write and to analyze more or less closely the words and sentences he is using. The tools employed are readers, writing books, spellers and grammars. The pedagogical value of these studies consists in the fact that by them we come in direct contact with all human learning and that they furnish the mind with the most natural and effective means for developing the powers of observation and reasoning. For the first three or four years the child is engaged in the mechanical processes of learning to read and write. When he can master the printed and the written word he is put to the acquisition of ideas through the literary selections he finds in his readers.

Now, what pedagogical value have religious studies in this phase of the student's development? I take it that the religious studies in the lowest grades are of the simplest description. They consist mainly in memorizing the prayers and in the acquisition of the formulæ which contain the essential truths of religion.

Of course, if your school is divided into water-tight compartments and religion is kept in one, this instruction has no influence either on reading or writing and has no pedagogical value beyond the exercise of the memory and whatever influence may be exerted on the will. But if the compartments are not water-tight, this religious instruction may, in the very lowest grades, supply the teacher with a most efficient instrument in developing the child's mind.

What is reading? It is the power of recognizing the word behind the symbol. This is the essence of reading, whether it is the power of reading Chinese or English. But we must read understandingly and the child is first put to recognizing the symbol for the common words of the language, the baby words, the words with which he is familiar.

The child's spoken vocabulary is therefore the first instrument for teaching reading.

But we all have two languages. There is the language of conversation and the language of literature. The one is the common vocabulary, the other is the elevated style. The object of reading is to introduce the child to the elevated style and to furnish him with the literary vocabulary. The difference after all between the educated man and the uneducated is chiefly made evident in the manner of speaking.

Now, here the religious teacher has from the very start an immense pedagogical advantage over the secular teacher. The latter is confined to the "cat and dog" and "bat and ball" vocabulary and the little things of child life, the former has already opened the child's ears to the mysterions voices of the tabernacle and taught him to answer, "Speak, Lord, for Thy servant heareth." Prayer is an elevation of the heart and it expresses itself in an elevated vocabulary. Side by side with the vocabulary of the common life which the Catholic child is acquiring with his secular brother, he is also learning a literary vocabulary by memorizing the prayers. The religious teacher, therefore, has two vocabularies to draw from in teaching reading and can the earlier furnish the child with examples of the elevated style.

But it is as the pupil advances in the elementary grades

that religious instruction becomes of unique pedagogical value in the teaching of language. From the earliest ages experience has shown that the most perfect instrument of literary education is the classic, the work in which the highest thoughts are expressed in a master's style. For that reason we teach the children from the lowest grades to read, to understand and often to commit to memory selections from the classic authors. By its terms the secular school is shut off from religion, and in all art religion is the inspiration of the best we have. But the domain of religion is open to the teacher of the religious school. Nay, more, if the religious school is to live up to its name, religion should be used for pedagogical purposes wherever and whenever it is possible to use it. Of course, if you mean by religious teaching a half hour's instruction in the catechism, while the rest of the day's program is just a reproduction of the public school curriculum, I will admit that you can do very little educational work with religion, either in the line of literature or in any other line. But if religious studies are barred from no hour of the school program, and if they are wisely used, they can be made of the highest utility, especially in the teaching of English literature.

The historical reason for that statement is that English literature, more than any other literature, is affected by one book and that a religious book, the Bible. The Bible was done into English at a time the language was forming and it has left an indelible impress upon the English speech. This is true of the Bible whether in the Douay or the Protestant version. The Douay, although the older in point of time, is younger in the point of language. It has been the fashion to criticize the Douay version because of its bad English, but where that criticism has not arisen from purely polemical motives it has come from a false notion of what good English really is, or from certain canons of taste about which there can be no disputing. Considering the Bible from the literary side, the differences between the Douay and the King James version are mostly superficial, and the former can be made as effectively as the latter an instrument for the formation of style.

But the Bible is an intensely religious book. So religious is it that the law has justly banished it from the secular school. Catholics rightly make a firm stand whenever the Bible is introduced into the public schools, even under the guise of a mere literary class book. If the Bible is to be used at all for any purpose it must first and foremost be used as a religious book.

Of course, when I speak of using the Bible in the school, I am not thinking of the old-fashioned Protestant idea that the whole Bible without note or comment should be put indiscriminately into children's hands. I am thinking of the use of selections from the Bible suitable to the age and mental development of the pupils.

To make my meaning clear I will take an imaginary school with an eight years' course. The children in the various grades have been taught and can recite selections from Longfellow and Scott, from Irving or Webster, or even from the writings of American or foreign Catholics. Yet, when I come to examine the children in this imaginary school, I find they have only the vaguest idea of that first and grandest of Christian poems, the *Magnificat* of the Mother of God, while they have no idea at all of Zachary's *Benedictus,* the swan song of the Ancient Dispensation. They know by heart what Mrs. Hemans wrote about the boy on the burning deck, but not a word have they of David's lament for Saul and Jonathan, or "The Lord is my Shepherd," or the heart-broken verses of the *Miserere.* Tennyson's sweet numbers are familiar to their ear, but the soul-haunting sayings of the Sermon on the Mount: "Behold the lilies of the field how they grow," the splendid simplicity of the parables by the Lake of Gallilec, the majestic march of the tragedy of the Passion—these things they know only as in a glass darkly, hearing them from the altar during the Sunday Mass or translated into the base language to which the writers of Bible histories seem to be condemned.

What a tremendous waste of opportunity in this imaginary religious school. Here is the school existing for the purpose of teaching religion. There is at hand religious instruction of the highest quality couched in language that at times makes it difficult for us to believe those who say that the very words were not dictated by the Holy Ghost. The instruction itself is eminently suited for children and is put in such a way that it captures their imagination and fires their wills while enlightening their understanding. They instinctively take to it as if their ears were still used to the voice of God walking in the garden of innocence. Now this religious instruction is also of the highest

value in forming literary style and cultivating literary
taste. Its pedagogical use is two-fold, religious and secular, and these uses are not antagonistic, but reinforce one
another. Yet our imaginary religious school leaves this
magnificent instrument to rust and proceeds to perform its
task with second-hand tools and worked-over materials.

APPENDIX D.

Catholic Educational Association Bulletin, Vol. IV, No. 1.
Report of the Proceedings and Addresses of the Fourth
Annual Meeting, Milwaukee, Wis., July 8-11, 1907. Pages
243-244:

The value of history as an instrument of education, even
of elementary education, is denied by none. But what is
the educational value of history? Does it consist in know-
ing strings of dates or lists of kings or the results of
sieges, battles, elections and the like? I am sure there is
little if any educational value in these things. The pedagogical value of history consists in this, that it broadens
the mind as one's horizon is broaded who stands upon a
mountain top and sees woods, fields, lakes, rivers, towns
lying between the everlasting ocean and the eternal hills.
But this view of the past is merely an unfixed photograph
unless we are taught to see the one increasing purpose
that runs through all the ages and how that men's thoughts
are widened with the process of the suns. History is
really the record of God's deeds through men. *Res gestae
Dei per homines.* It is from history taught in this manner
that we obtain the true solution of the records of the past;
it offers the only hope of reading the riddle of the future.

Yet what history can begin to compare with the Bible
history and Church history for qualities such as these?
Bible history itself was written under divine inspiration
precisely for the purpose of recording the manner by which
God's merciful design for the redemption of man was ac-
complished, first the blade, then the ear, then the full corn
in the ear.

As in elementary schools we cannot begin with formal
history until the final years; we are compelled to introduce
the study of history by stories, wonder tales, biographies
and the like. There is no history that lends itself to this
treatment like Bible history. The stories of the infancy

of our Lord have a wonderful attraction for children. They will listen to them forever and reproduce them with delight. At a very early age they learn to love the history of the sacred Passion and to walk with our Savior from Gethsemani to Calvary. The Old Testament is packed with material. The Garden of Paradise, Cain and Abel, the Deluge, the Patriarchs, the story of Joseph, Moses, the Judges, the Kings, Elias and Eliseus, the prophets of Juda, the Exile, the Machabees, Peter, and Stephen, and Paul, this is the history by which the world was molded into the form of Christian civilization and beside it there is no finer or better tempered pedagogical instrument to hand.

There is just one remark I would make about the teaching of Bible history in the elementary schools, and that is that it should be as far as possible in the words of the Bible. I do not believe, as I have already said, that the Bible should be used as a text-book, but whatever text-book is used should be couched in the *ipsissima verba* of the sacred volume. Moreover, such chronology as is introduced should be of the most general description, and especial care should be taken to keep from the minds of the children the idea that the Church or the truth of God's revelation is bound up with any of the numerous systems of Biblical chronology that learned men have devised.

APPENDIX E.

A Practical Commentary on Holy Scripture, by Frederick Justus Knecht, D. D. Herder, St. Louis. Preface to English translation, by Rev. Michael F. Glancey. Pages xiv, xv, xvi, xvii, xviii, xix:

Leaving the domain of general Catechetics, we now come to that branch which is the subject-matter of the present volume, viz. Bible History. And, first of all, it may be asked: What place does Bible History hold in a course of religious instruction? Bible History is not the foundation on which religious instruction rests, nor the centre round which it revolves, nor the goal towards which it tends. Our religion centres in our faith, which is not a condensed extract from Bible History, but comes from the Church. Not Bible History, then, but the teaching of the Church, must, on Catholic principles, be at once the beginning, middle and end of religious instruction. Hence Bible History, to claim a place in religious instruction, must do so only inasmuch as it bears on the doctrines of faith. If this principle be kept steadily in view, Bible History may be made to render most valuable service in religious instruction. The illustrative light it throws on doctrinal truths makes them more easily intelligible. They become invested with a concrete form, are clothed with flesh and blood, breathe the breath of life, and move like living truths before our eyes. In the Cathechism, they appear as cold abstracts and mere outlines. Thus Bible History becomes an object-lesson in faith, a veritable pictorial Cathechism. How powerfully, for instance, is the truth of an all-ruling Providence illustrated by the histories of Joseph and Abraham! What, again, is better calculated to teach the power of prayer than the stories of Moses praying while the Israelites fought, and of the Church praying for the imprisoned Peter? On the other hand, the fate of Judas and the rejection of Juda show forth, in all their hideous deformity, the terrible consequences of resistance to grace; while the history of the fall of Eve and of Peter brings out the necessity of avoiding dangerous occasions. In this way, Bible History at once proves and illustrates doctrinal truth. And it likewise develops and expands such truth. The Catechism tells us, indeed, how and why Christ suffered, but Bible History gives a full and detailed account of His sufferings, and so enables us better to realize the infinite love of God and the enormity of sin. The texts of Scripture that in the Catechism stand isolated and shorn of their context, are now seen in the light of their surroundings and speak to us with a new force and meaning. Moreover, Bible History serves to complete the Catechism. The Catechism, for example, is silent about miracles, about God's mercy and forbearance, His patience and long-suffering. Of humility, and indeed of many other virtues, it is also silent, except that it arranges them over against the opposing vices. But would we learn their nature and properties, and how pleasing they are to God, it is to Bible History that we must turn. The Catechism is monosyllabic in stating the duties that children owe to their parents, masters to their servants, and vice versa; whereas the history of the centurion's servant, of Heli's sons, and of Tobias surrounds these duties with a halo of interpreting light. Again, Bible History exhibits religious truth in its bearing and action on the most varied states and conditions. Virtue and vice stand before us, with life-blood coursing through their veins, in attractive beauty or repellent ugliness. The Good Samaritan invites to mercy; Job, in his resignation to God's will, is a beacon-light to the sorrowing; the Apostles going forth from the scourges, and rejoicing that they were accounted worthy to suffer for Christ, invest with a startling reality the beatitude: Blessed are they that suffer persecution for justice' sake.

From all this it is clear that Bible History is not to be read, as too often it is, merely as a story-book; that it is to be studied, not on its own account, but because it imparts life and vigour, picturesqueness and comprehensiveness to religious instruction; because it elucidates, proves, enforces and illustrates the truths that go to make up religious instruction. But, as Dr. Knecht insists, in order that Bible History may be in a position to render these services, it must be "taught in the closest connexion with the Catechism". "Catechism and Bible History must mutually interpenetrate [*"In inniger gegenseitiger Durchdringung"*], for only in this way is a systematic course of religious instruction possible" (p. 9). Catechism and Bible History must go hand in hand, but Catechism must be in the van. Catechism is the guiding principle, and Bible History its handmaid.

These are the principles, weighty though elementary, on which Dr. Knecht and all writers on Catechetics are generally agreed. And how does practice harmonize with principles? Is practice attuned to principle? Or are the two in hopeless discord? To begin with, how many teachers have mastered the reason why Bible History has a place in religious instruction? How many, or how few, realize the fact that Bible History and Catechism should be "taught in the closest connexion"? And what percentage of those who have grasped this truth put it in practice? There is no denying the patent fact that, as a rule, the two are not taught concurrently, and are not made to run on parallel lines. Ten to one, the Bible History set down for a class in a given year has no connexion whatever with the doctrinal instruction of that year. Thus, while children are being instructed in the Holy Eucharist, their Scripture History turns on that singularly uninspiring period embraced by the reigns of the kings of Israel and Juda! All this comes from being enslaved to the chronological system. This is the root of the evil to which the axe must be laid. Forgetting the plain principle that should underlie the teaching of all Bible History, and utterly ignoring the profit or loss to the children, we have stumbled over the crooked idea that Bible History must be taught chronologically even in our poor schools. I am far from denying, nay, I affirm that a systematic course of Bible History should be given when time and facilities are not wanting, as in our upper schools and colleges. But in our poor schools, where the time barely suffices to give the necessary instruction and to drive it home with religious effect, a slavish adhesion to chronology is to sacrifice realities to figures. To talk of a systematic course in this sense, under such circumstances, is nothing short of preposterous. In the chronological system, Bible History cannot, except by a happy accident, enforce and illustrate the religious instruction. Far from being a help, it is a drawback. Instead of elucidating, it obscures. No longer the handmaid, it seeks to be on an equality with the mistress. For religious instruction to succeed in its great purpose, it must, as Dr. Knecht rightly says, be conducted on a "unitive" plan. The unit is the doctrinal instruction, with which the Bible History must be brought into line, unless we are to fly in the teeth of all our principles. Let me now briefly illustrate what I mean by this unification or concentration of subject that I am advocating, lest perhaps I be twitted with pulling down without attempting to build up. Instead, therefore, of teaching children who are being instructed in the Blessed Eucharist about the kings of Israel and Juda, I would teach them the Scripture History of the Blessed Eucharist, as in the following plan [From *Scripture History for Schools* (No. 3). Approved for use in the Diocese of Birmingham]:

THE HOLY EUCHARIST.

I. Types of the Holy Eucharist:
    1. The Sacrifice of Melchisedech.
    2. The Paschal Lamb.
    3. The Manna.
    4. The Food of Elias.
    5. The Jewish Sacrifices.

II. The Prophecy of Malachias.

III. Christ promises a new Sacrifice:
    1. At Jacob's Well,
    2. After the multiplication of the loaves.

IV. The Last Supper.—Institution of the Blessed Eucharist.

V. The two disciples going to Emmaus.

VI. Miracles illustrative of the Blessed Eucharist:
1. Water made wine at Cana.
2. Multiplication of loaves.
3. Christ walking on the waters.
4. The Transfiguration.

The important subject of the Church may be treated somewhat similarly.

THE CHURCH.

Part I. The Old Testament.

I. Introductory.

II. The Church a Family.
1. Noe. The Ark.
2. Call of Abraham.—The promises to Abraham, Isaac and Jacob.

III. The Church a People.
1. Moses.
2. Giving of the Law.
3. The Tabernacle.
4. Entrance into Promised Land.

IV. The Church a Kingdom.
1. David.
2. Solomon.—Building of the Temple.
3. The kingdom broken up.

V. God promises to set up a New Kingdom.

Part II. The Gospels.

VI. Introductory.

VII. Christ the King.—The Kingdom of God.

VIII. Parables on the kingdom of God.
1. The Hidden Treasure.
2. The Pearl of Great Price.
3. The Wheat and the Cockle.
4. The Drag-net.
5. The Leaven.
6. The Mustard Seed.
7. The Good Shepherd.

IX. Jesus calls Disciples.

Appendices.

In a word, the Scripture History should be grouped round the central doctrines of our faith.

APPENDIX F.

Tracts, Theological and Ecclesiastical. By John Henry Cardinal Newman. Longmans: 1899. The Rheims and Douay Versions of Holy Scripture, page 410.

Such is the history of the Rheims and Douay Bible, of which there have been two editions of the Old Testament, 1609-10 and 1635, and eight (including the New York Protestant reprint) of the New—1582, 1600, 1621, 1633, 1738, 1788, 1816-1818, and 1834. This version comes to us on the authority of certain divines of the Cathedral and College of Rheims and of the University of Douay, confirmed by the subsequent indirect recognition of English, Scotch and Irish Bishops, and by its general reception by the faithful. It never has had any episcopal *imprimatur,* much less has it received any formal approbation from the Holy See.

Appendices.

APPENDIX G.

"Teaching of Liturgy." Paper by Father Yorke at the Catholic Educational Conference at Buffalo, 1917. Extract:

These suggestions are not mere theories. I have been working on them for over twenty years, and, while I have not always or everywhere attained my ideal, still the results have met with approval from priests, teachers and parents interested in such matters. Indeed, the most serious criticism I have heard was from a Bishop after Confirmation —that it was too perfect.

Therefore, I will not set them forth as the abstract proposals of a course of studies, but will simply tell in narrative form what I do, giving my reasons why, where they may not be self-apparent.

My apparatus consists of a little pamphlet of 46 pages, bound in paper and selling for a few cents. It is published in this cheap form because by Christmas it has usually shared the fate of the penny Catechism, and the boys especially have twisted, turned and tortured it into all kinds of shapes, and have developed an almost diabolic ingenuity in secreting it in the most unexpected and inaccessible parts of their garments. In order that you may be better able to follow me, I have sent a few dozen copies to be distributed among you. The children know it as the Mass Book.

Half the book, from page 10 to 34, is taken up with the Order of the Mass. I notice that even the new English Missals stick to the "Ordinary of the Mass," which is not Roman. Our Missal has Ordo Missae, not Ordinarium Missae. I put the Order of the Mass not at the beginning of the book, but in the middle—first, because that is the place it occupies in the authorized Missal, reminding us that Sunday is the weekly observance of the Resurrection, and because, to reach the Proper, you have to turn only half the number of pages, and, last, but not least, because it is easier on the binding. In that Order of the Mass there is only what is in the Missal with the rubrics, of course, practically excised.

As in the Roman Missal, the book begins with the Proper of the Masses of the season—first, Advent, then Christmas, then Epiphany, followed by Septuagesima and Lent. After the Order of the Mass, we have, on page 35, Easter, then

Appendices.

Ascesion and Pentecost, with Masses for Trinity, Corpus Christi, Blessed Virgin, Confirmation and First Communion; the last two are, of course, extra-Liturgical, but very useful.

If you examine these Masses you will see that they are all built on a uniform system. First, a seasonable hymn called the Introit, a second hymn or anthem called the Gradual, a third hymn called the Offertory, and a fourth hymn called the Communion. These hymns are not, of course, the Liturgical Introits and Graduals, but they are sung at the Introit or Gradual of the Mass, and the title makes the children familiar with the proper names of these parts of the Mass. I would call your attention to the fact that I have made the Communion an anthem of the Blessed Virgin, and that there is always one Latin hymn either in the proper or in the common.

You know that in the Mass there are three lines of prayers—first, the Sacrificial Prayers proper to the priest as sacrificer, such as the Preface and the Canon; secondly, Personal Devotional Prayers proper to the priest as an individual, such as the Forty-second Psalm and the Confession; thirdly, the Prayers belonging to the people or the choir, such as the Introit, Kyrie, Gloria, Credo, and the rest. Now, my object is to have the children sing or recite in English what a college choir in a Gregorian Mass would chant in Latin, remembering always that in the Proper we have adapted hymns not the Liturgical Introits, Graduals, etc.

If you will begin at page 10, we will run briefly through the Mass. The children assemble in church at the hour for their Mass, and, kneeling down, they make their preparation, which consists of what the priest recites at the foot of the altar. Sometimes a priest may act as reader, sometimes a teacher, sometimes a parishioner. All that is necessary is that he read slowly and clearly, and keep his wits about him. He should have nothing to do with the discipline of the children, as his office of reader will need his whole attention.

Having finished the Preparation, the organ gives the tune for the Introit, and at that signal the celebrant enters the sanctuary; the children stand and immediately begin the Introit hymn. When the celebrant has arranged the chalice, and has come to the foot of the altar (which should be done in the interval between the first and second verses), the children kneel and continue the hymn. By the time the celebrant has read the Introit, the children have finished, and immediately the reader begins, "Lord, have mercy," which is continued alternately by the boys and the girls. In like manner, the Gloria is said, the celebrant timing himself not to go ahead of the children—a difficult task in the beginning, especially for nervous persons.

After the Gloria the reader recites the Collect from his Missal, and then follows with the Epistle for the day. By this time the celebrant has finished the Gradual, and while the book is changed, the children rise and sing their Gradual verse. After the Gospel the celebrant turns to the children, reads the Gospel in English, makes the announcements, and gives the instruction.

The reader begins with the celebrant, "I believe in one God," which the boys and girls continue alternately. Here it will be especially necessary for the celebrant to time himself so that he may not genuflect at the Incarnatus before the children have come to it. During the Offertory the children sing their hymn, and the reader begins the Preface with the celebrant. The children recite the "Sanctus," and there is silence until after the Elevation, when they sing a hymn to the Blessed Sacrament.

The "Our Father" is recited in chorus, and the "Agnus Dei" by the boys and girls alternately. At the "Domine Non Sum Dignus" they may sing three times the little hymn, "O Lord, I am not worthy." Then they sing the anthem set for the Communion; the reader recites the Post Communion, and there is silence to the end of the Mass, when they sing a hymn of thanksgiving.

You see at once that the children are kept going all the time, and all the time they are following with the priest. You see, too, it requires almost perfect drill, because if this way of attending Mass is not done with precision it degenerates rapidly into a riot. *Corruptio optimi pessima.*

I begin with the school year, which is the season after Pentecost. This is the longest of all the seasons, and gives us a good chance to ground ourselves in the work without having the frequent changes in the hymns proper to the other seasons. You will note, too, on page 38, that the hymns prescribed are easy and familiar, so that even at the very first year we can get good results. Then I divide the prayers amongst the grades. The First Grade learns to read the "Our Father," the "Kyrie," the short responses and the "Agnus Dei," together with the hymns, "Angel of God," "O Lord, I am not worthy," etc. In the Second Grade, in addition, they learn the "Sanctus," their part of the "Gloria," and the answers to Psalm 42. In the hymns they can take nearly all the Introits. In the Third Grade they learn to read the Nicene Creed and the Gospel of St. John, and a select number of hymns. In the Fourth Grade they read and get a general explanation of the Offertory Prayers and the Canon, and they should now know by heart all their own part of the Mass. All this can be done by giving steady and systematic instruction for five minutes every day in the school. Of course, I take it for granted that the teaching of the hymns is taken up in the regular singing period, and that wherever there may be reading, parsing, analysis, etc., they come in the language period.

Then, on Friday afternoon, I bring the children into the church and put them through the Mass. Continual care has to be given to prevent them from drawling the hymns and galloping through the prayers. After three or four weeks, the drill is pretty well understood, and I take up parts of the Mass, such as the Gloria or Credo, and give a special practice on reading them reverently and intelligently. Later on, as the seasons change, I explain their significance and the meaning of the hymns. Through it I intersperse now on one day, now on another, short instruction on the Church, the altar, the vestments, and the like. Before Communion and Confirmation I have found it valuable and interesting to the children to take them into the sacristy and sanctuary, and show them at close range the altar and its ornaments. Some people object to this, as leading to irreverence, but I have never found it so if the matter is properly handled.

or to the

NORTHERN REGIONAL LIBRARY FACILITY
Bldg. 400, Richmond Field Station
University of California
Richmond, CA 94804-4698

ALL BOOKS MAY BE RECALLED AFTER 7 DAYS
2-month loans may be renewed by calling
   (415) 642-6233
1-year loans may be recharged by bringing books
   to NRLF
Renewals and recharges may be made 4 days
   prior to due date

CPSIA information can be obtained
at www.ICGtesting.com
Printed in the USA
BVHW081730201118
533619BV00008B/518/P

9 780483 135307